Superfast
CARS

by Mark Dubowski

Consultant: Paul F. Johnston, Washington, D.C.

BEARPORT
PUBLISHING COMPANY, INC.

New York, New York

Credits
Cover and title page, Auto Imagery; 4, courtesy, NHRA Media Center; 5, Jim Kelly / Match Race Madness Archive; 6-7, Jon Asher; 8, Bonniwellphotography.com; 9, AP / Wide World Photos; 10, Auto Imagery; 11, Buzz Pictures, Alamy; 12–13, Auto Imagery; 14, Ken Weddle; 15, AP / Wide World Photos; 16-17, John Ewald / wdifl.com; 18-19, Auto Imagery; 20, Steve Reyes; 21, Leatha Robinson; 22, 23, 24, 25, Auto Imagery; 26, Nik Wheeler / Corbis; 27, Michael Kim; 29, Auto Imagery.

Editorial development by Judy Nayer
Design & Production by Paula Jo Smith

Special thanks to Peggy Hunnewell at the Don Garlits Museum of Drag Racing

Library of Congress Cataloging-in-Publication Data

Dubowski, Mark.
  Superfast cars / by Mark Dubowski.
      p. cm.—(Ultimate speed)
  Includes bibliographical references and index.
  ISBN 1-59716-080-6 (library binding)—ISBN 1-59716-117-9 (pbk.)
  1. Automobiles, Racing—Juvenile literature. I. Title. II. Series.

  TL236.D83 2006
  629.228—dc22

                    2005009753

For more information, write to Bearport Publishing Company, Inc., 101 Fifth Avenue, Suite 6R, New York, New York 10003. Printed in the United States of America.

3 4 5 6 7 8 9 10

CONTENTS

Big Daddy

His name is Don Garlits, but everyone calls him "Big Daddy." In the world of drag racing, he is a **legend**. In 1957, he became the first drag racer to go faster than 170 miles per hour (274 kph). In 1964, he became the first drag racer to go 200 miles per hour (322 kph).

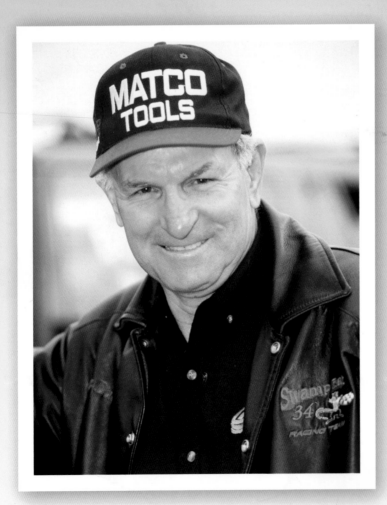

Don "Big Daddy" Garlits

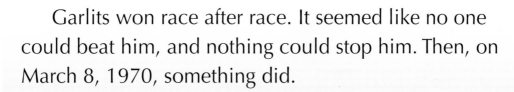

Garlits won race after race. It seemed like no one could beat him, and nothing could stop him. Then, on March 8, 1970, something did.

The racetrack for drag racing is only a little longer than a football field. It amazed people that Garlits could hit top speed in such a short distance.

Garlits named his drag race cars Swamp Rat. His first car was Swamp Rat I (1), his second was Swamp Rat II (2), and so on. Garlits is shown here in 1970 racing Swamp Rat XIII (13).

A Noise Like a Bomb

Garlits was racing at the Lions Drag Strip in Long Beach, California. The Swamp Rat was lined up next to Richard Tharp's car. The **starter** turned on the starting lights, known as the "Christmas tree." First, one yellow light appeared. Then two more yellow lights glowed.

The crowd watched in shock as Don Garlits's Swamp Rat exploded.

The green light was about to go on, when Tharp hit the gas too soon. His front wheels crossed the starting line early. He was **disqualified**.

Garlits took off on time, but he didn't finish the race. As soon as he crossed the starting line, his car blew up. It sounded like a bomb going off.

The Lions Drag Strip opened in 1955. Don Garlits's accident was one of its most famous. The drag strip closed in 1972.

Disaster!

Underneath the Swamp Rat, the **gearbox** had exploded. The blast ripped the car in half. The rear end spun around, smoking, with Garlits inside.

Car parts flew everywhere. Two people in the stands were hit. One almost died. The other person's arm was cut off. Garlits was knocked out cold.

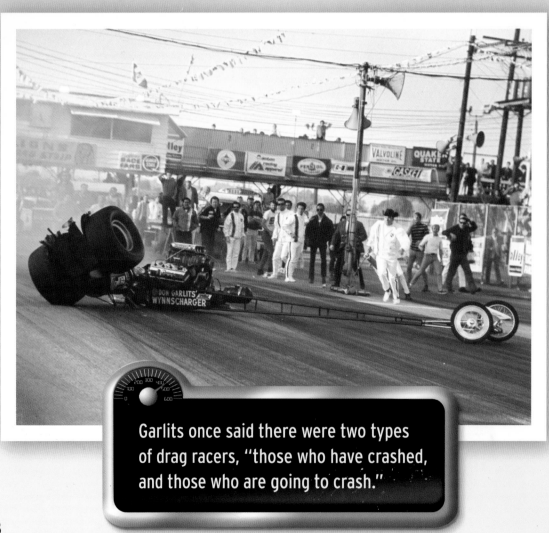

Garlits once said there were two types of drag racers, "those who have crashed, and those who are going to crash."

When he woke up, Garlits did not know what had happened. The emergency crew rushed to the car and pulled him out. Garlits was alive, but the front half of his right foot was blown off.

Drag racing is hard on engines. It is easy for parts to break, explode, or catch on fire.

Drag Racing in the Beginning

Drag racing was created to take the place of **illegal** street racing. In street racing, two cars met side-by-side at a traffic light or other starting line. When the light turned green, both cars took off in a race to see which one was faster.

The Super Street dragster looks like a normal car—until it takes off.

The National Hot Rod Association (NHRA) said street racing was dangerous to racers and other drivers. So, they came up with the drag strip. This track was a straight quarter-mile (.4 km) and had two lanes. Instead of racing from a traffic light, dragsters (drag race cars) on the drag strip took off from the starting light. Suddenly, street racing had become a legal sport.

In demo derby, drivers smash other cars, hoping to wreck them so they cannot finish. In some countries this type of racing is called banger racing.

The Early Days

Early dragsters were called "slingshots" because they took off so fast. In these cars, the driver sat behind the engine.

This slingshot driver is doing a "burnout." He is spinning the rear wheels to melt rubber onto the track. A burnout gives the driver extra traction when he takes off.

Dragsters can hit higher speeds than other race cars because of the track, or drag strip, they run on. Race cars on an oval track must slow down as they make turns. A drag strip has no turns. Unlike a rally track, a drag strip is flat, so there are no hills to go up. In other races, drivers must go around other cars to win. The dragster has a clear road from start to finish.

Races are held at drag strips all over the United States. Each year, the NHRA oversees more than 50 championship races.

Drag strip in Pomona, California

Old Wounds

The crash in Long Beach was not the first time Don Garlits had been in an accident. Ten years earlier, a Swamp Rat engine had caught on fire. Garlits almost died. He had **third-degree burns** and was in the hospital for weeks.

An early Swamp Rat

When Garlits **recovered**, he wanted to do something to make drag racing safer. He asked Jim Deist, an expert in airplane and pilot safety, for help. Together, the men came up with a new kind of suit that protected racers against engine fires. It was called the **flame-retardant** suit.

Drag racing suits keep many drivers from getting killed.

A drag racer's helmet is called a "brain bucket."

The Promise: A Safer Car

Garlits decided that the flame-retardant suit was not enough protection. Before he would race again, he would make a safer drag race car.

Garlits and the first rear-engine dragster

Many racers had tried to put the car engine behind the driver. So far, it hadn't worked. When tested, the drivers always over-steered and lost control. However, Garlits, along with another racer named Connie Swingle, solved the problem. They made the wheel harder to turn.

In 1971, Garlits drove a truck into **the pits** at the NHRA Winternationals in California. Behind him, on a **trailer**, was the new rear-engine dragster.

The "big race" in drag racing is the Winternationals. Every year over 55,000 people come to watch.

RED: Rear-Engine Design

The number one cause of serious injuries in drag racing used to be engine fires. A hot engine and **explosive** fuel could be a deadly combination. As the wind blew the fire back, the driver would be covered in flames.

Rear-engine dragsters at the 2005 NHRA National Event in Phoenix, Arizona

With the engine behind the driver, the flames would be in back of the car. The driver should be in a safer position if a fire occurred. Everyone was eager to see what Garlits's new rear-engine dragster could do.

There may be hundreds of dragsters at an event, but cars race only two at a time. The winner then races against another car.

Drag Racing Changes Forever

Garlits's rear-engine car was small, but fast. The Swamp Rat XIV (14) won race after race. By the end of the day, the world of drag racing had changed forever.

Race car shops were flooded with orders for the rear-engine design. Garlits's Swamp Rat XIV brought the age of the slingshot to a close.

The Swamp Rat XIV changed the way dragsters were built.

These dragsters were about the same length as slingshots. However, their engines were bigger and stronger.

A few years later, Don Garlits had another idea. His new invention would lead to even more powerful engines and faster speeds.

The world speed record for dragsters is 319.4 miles per hour (514 kph). It was set by Chuck Haynes on April 6, 2002, in a jet-powered dragster.

The Swamp Rat XV (15) was never raced. It was built as a backup, just in case the Swamp Rat XIV didn't work.

Cars with Wings

At the 1963 Winternationals, Garlits had rolled out a Swamp Rat that had a wing mounted over the engine. It worked like an airplane wing, only backwards. Instead of creating **lift**, it pressed the car down, pushing the tires flat on the road. The wing gave the dragster more **friction**, which helped the car reach greater speeds.

Burning rubber from the tires makes a cloud of smoke.

Soon, other dragsters and race cars started using wings. With a big wing to hold the car on the road, new rear-engine dragster engines could be bigger and stronger than ever.

Shirley Muldowney (above) is one of only a few female drag racers. She is also one of the top racers of all time and holds many world records.

Drag racing is one of the only sports in the world in which women and girls compete on an even basis with men and boys.

Wheelie!

Today, rear-engine design and the wing are typical equipment on dragsters. However, some things have not changed from the days of the slingshot. Large rear tires provide the extra friction needed to grip the track. The front tires can be small because there is very little friction needed for steering on a straight track.

A Super Stock Car doing a wheelie

Sometimes, when the dragster takes off, the front wheels lift off the ground in a wheelie. A wheelie bar behind the back wheels has a pair of tiny wheels that stop the car from lifting too high.

Some dragsters complete an entire race in less than six seconds.

A wheelie bar on a Pro Stock Car

A Racing Legend

Don Garlits began racing in 1950. He won his first major victory in 1955. Since that time, he has won 144 **national** events, including 17 World Championships.

Visitors can see Don Garlits's cars up close at his Museum of Drag Racing in Ocala, Florida.

Winning, however, did not always come easy to Garlits. He was badly burned in an engine fire. He lost half his foot in an explosion. Still, Garlits did not give up. He designed the flame-retardant suit so drivers would not be burned. He perfected the rear-engine design so explosions would not easily set the drivers on fire. By turning problems into victories, Don Garlits became a true racing legend.

The Indycar tracks are tilted to keep the cars from flying off the road.

JUST THE FACTS More About Drag Racing

- There are different stories about how the term "drag racing" came about. Some say it's because people would say to each other, "Drag your car out of the garage and race me." Others say the name has to do with where the races took place. The "main drag" of a town was the main street. This street was the only one wide enough for two cars to fit side by side.

- Don Garlits, "King of the dragsters," won the NHRA U.S. Nationals a record eight times. In 2001, at the age of 69, Garlits returned to drag racing to make his first 300-mile per hour (483-kph) run in a Top Fuel dragster.

- From a standing start, Top Fuel dragsters are the fastest-accelerating vehicles in the world. They cover the quarter-mile (.4-km) race in 4.4 seconds at speeds faster than 300 miles per hour (483 kph).

TIMELINE

This timeline shows some important events in the history of drag racing.

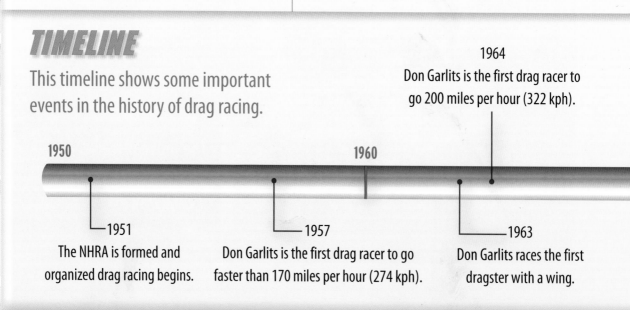

1964
Don Garlits is the first drag racer to go 200 miles per hour (322 kph).

1950

1960

1951
The NHRA is formed and organized drag racing begins.

1957
Don Garlits is the first drag racer to go faster than 170 miles per hour (274 kph).

1963
Don Garlits races the first dragster with a wing.

- Shirley Muldowney was the sport's first three-time world champion.

- One of the biggest car races is the Formula One Grand Prix. Millions of people around the world watch the race on television. "Grand Prix" is French for "Big Prize." Top racers earn millions of dollars.

Shirley Muldowney

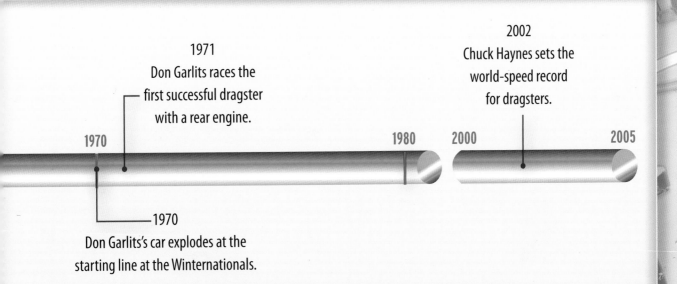

1971
Don Garlits races the first successful dragster with a rear engine.

2002
Chuck Haynes sets the world-speed record for dragsters.

1970   1980   2000   2005

1970
Don Garlits's car explodes at the starting line at the Winternationals.

GLOSSARY

disqualified (diss-KWOL-uh-fyed) prevented from taking part in an activity for breaking a rule or rules

explosive (ek-SPLOH-siv) able or likely to blow up

flame-retardant (FLAYM ri-TAR-dent) resistant to catching fire

friction (FRIK-shuhn) the force that slows down objects when they are rubbing against each other

gearbox (GIHR-boks) the part of a car that controls the power between the engine and the axle and wheels

illegal (i-LEE-guhl) against the law

legend (LEJ-uhnd) a person whose life story is remembered for many years

lift (LIFT) the upward force caused by air passing over and under a wing

national (NASH-uh-nuhl) having to do with the whole country

recovered (ri-KUHV-urd) got better after an illness or injury

starter (STAR-tur) the person who signals the beginning of a race

the pits (THUH PITS) the place near a racetrack where crews work on cars

third-degree burns (THURD duh-GREE BUHRNZ) the worst kind of skin burns, in which all layers of the skin are destroyed

trailer (TRAYL-ur) a vehicle pulled by a car or truck

BIBLIOGRAPHY

speedtalk.com/shows/016_garlits_lehman.html
www.americanjetcars.com/sitemap.htm
www.competitionplus.com/2004_11_18/cowin.html
www.deist.com
www.dragraceresults.com
www.garlits.com
www.muldowney.com

READ MORE

Jefferis, David. *Race Cars.* Minneapolis, MN: Sagebrush Books (2003).

Kelley, K.C. *NASCAR Racing to the Finish.* Pleasantville, NY: Reader's Digest (2005).

Kulling, Monica. *Eat My Dust! Henry Ford's First Race.* New York: Random House (2004).

Lord, Trevor. *Big Book of Race Cars.* New York: DK Publishing (2001).

Piehl, Janet. *Formula One Race Cars.* Minneapolis, MN: Lerner Publications (2004).

Pitt, Matthew. *Drag Racer.* Danbury, CT: Children's Press (2001).

Simon, Seymour. *Cool Cars.* New York: SeaStar Books (2004).

LEARN MORE ONLINE

Visit these Web sites to learn more about superfast cars:
www.autoracing.about.com
www.formula1.com/insight/technicalinfo/11/468.html
www.indycar.com
www.nhra.com

INDEX

ABOUT THE AUTHOR

Mark Dubowski has written and illustrated many
books for young readers. He lives in North Carolina.